Toward a

Toward a Catalogue of Falling

Méira Cook

Brick Books

CANADIAN CATALOGUING IN PUBLICATION DATA

Cook, Méira, 1964-
    Toward a catalogue of falling

Poems.
ISBN 0-919626-88-2

    I. Title.

PS8555.O567T68 1996   C811'.54   C96-931595-3
PR9199.3.C66T68 1996

Copyright © Méira Cook, 1996.

The support of the Canada Council and the Ontario Arts Council is gratefully acknowledged.

Cover is after a photograph by the author.

Typeset in Trump Mediaeval. Printed and bound by The Porcupine's Quill. The stock is acid-free Zephyr Antique laid.

Brick Books
431 Boler Road, Box 20081
London, Ontario
N6K 4G6

To my parents, Chana and Chonie
and to Aviva

אם אין אני לי, מי לי

וּכשאני לעצמי, מה אני

Contents

Diptych I   9
Diptych II   11

Legends of Tongue
    In Pendulum of Green   15
    Too Ripe for Skin   16
    Legends of Tongue   17
    Slip of the Tongue I   18
    Slip of the Tongue II   19
    Slip of the Tongue III   20
    Last Fall   21

The Ruby Garrote
    gaudy she stands on one leg   25
    petco the ringmaster stares at the world   26
    rosie envies the stability of tables   27
    the clowns are dying all over the world   28
    rosie hunkers in her body   29
    the beast has found me out at last   30
    you are going to have to let   31
    always announced in the dark   32
    let's us two go halvsies   33
    amongst her mirrors my lady   34
    four lions trained but not tamed   35

The Fallen Here
    Fairytales from the Old Country   39
    Any Old Skin   41
    Fooling the Jasmine   42
    The Fallen Here   43
    Such a Long Way   45

String Quartet
    Prima parte moderato   49
    Seconda parte allegro   50
    Recapitulazione della prima parte moderato   51
    Coda legato molto   52

Days of Water   53

For Breath & Glass
    All Day   67
    When you open a door in a street   69
    Here in Venice   70
    Toward a Catalogue of Falling   72
    Vertical cities   75
    Some Place   76

Epigrams for Breath & Glass   77

Elsewhere
    Light, moving   87
    Worn Through   89
    Various Blues   91
    Into Category   93
    Water, falling   95
    Reading Oranges   97
    Following Herself   99

Triptych
    Rumours of Bear   103
    Like Rain   106
    Bestiary in Three Parts   108

Diptych 1

According to Brueghel when Icarus fell it was spring.
William Carlos Williams

Perhaps it is always spring
when we fall.

The first is easy, a gush
of green the blood
rising in high chambers
like sap. It is the other
that confounds
the falling.

To fall
in love asleep downstairs
of those three I have fallen
twice. The one is gentle
a laying on of hands, the other
hard my body clicking
open and shut, a turnstile.
But I have never fallen
as Icarus
from grace.

Poor Icarus who suffered
from *hubris* and *oedipus*
in equal measure, now
there is a fall for you.
Imagine wanting to please

daddy and snub god
at the same time.

No wonder he spun
into that blank ocean wax
dripping from the blades
of shoulders, legs scissoring
the seam of sea and sky.

But it was spring when Icarus
                              fell
in love asleep downstairs
and out of the sky.

We have his legs to remember this by.

Diptych 11

*In Brueghel's Icarus, for instance; how everything
turns away
Quite leisurely from the disaster.*
                    W. H. Auden

I turn and walk (quite leisurely)
from the canvas by
that mocking passionate com-
passionate man who painted
lepers and whores, burghermen
tax-collectors and fishwives
wet-lashed cripples
on the margins of the crowd
feast days and plunderings
interchangeably and the odd
rape as well as a pair
of well-shaped calves
kicking out negligently
from a painted ocean.

I turn and walk
away, you turn
with me the guard
who has been examining
your well-shaped calves
turns the better to hide
his wet-lashed eyes.

I turn you turn he
turns, behind
our turned backs
two well-shaped calves
kick out negligently
from a painted ocean.

Legends of Tongue

In Pendulum of Green

At the parabola of day
in the garden's thickest
pause, girl swings in pendulum of
green too deep for colour green
is sound, a gush of leaves
cells fractured in light.

Close your eyes against the sun
watch the skin imprinted red
on the filter of your eye feel
desire deep as colour, here red
is disease heatsickness home
sickness and the slick unease of

love in a red country green as blood
girl rocks herself over the hump
of midday while the garden
brawls in shadow while the sun
flowers in root of eye.
Swing high swing low she sings

her soul's pale exile from this
bright gash of earth. Here fruit
and dust and snake is red,
spider and tongue and nail and
word. Only memory is green
a garden, and dies every year.

Too Ripe for Skin

The smell of ferment is a colour also
on the inside of colour, the ooze
of plums too ripe for their skins
heatblown in dust at the garden's
meridian. Sun pours us out honey
sluggish in slow time, already
ants crawl in the crevice of toes.

I have eaten myself fat on
the garden, sun sops me up olive
oil soaked through bread. It was
you who said, *too ripe for skin*.

Put the garden to your ear, listen.
The ferment of things grown to seed
and rot is colour also. The suck
slide of worm through cavities
of earth of flesh, maggot colour
rainbows in the bowels blooms
buds and blows in the eye.

Unzip unzip, there is a catch
between my thighs here let me
uncolour myself for you, peel
my legs like stockings.

Legends of Tongue

Caged behind teeth tongue outpaces
her captivity in words, stories
herself pliant and profane, squawks
the dark world to tattletale and rag

first

was the world the edible garden, then
snake wriggled south leaving word only
of scales gathering in the place of
god, a language grown to the girth of

trees

also stars.
Words branched and antlered
fall to furrow two by two, it was
the catalogue that arked them in the

end

against the grind of Ararat. No loss
of creature fossilled in print not
gone if one slant letter arched in sky
remains.

Slip of the Tongue 1

If you want to catch wolf first
take your hunting knife, rub grease
on the blade. Wolf will come cut
her tongue to the root taste the
blood, sucksuck at her own salt
source, greedy for the insides
of things. A trackless pacing
wells slowly to the throat is
swallowed in one gulp wolf drinks
wolf, pours her body clotted out
cup and knife will serve you well
if you want to catch wolf. Look
how she lies mouth open tongue
dry at last, she has swallowed
herself twice already gnawed
down to the quick to the nub
to the root of tongue. There is
another trick to be learnt

if you want to catch crow.

Slip of the Tongue 11

If you want to catch crow first
lime your tree, here comes
crow. He will stick out his tongue
ho-ho he is caught, now
you can teach him to speak. Say
feather crow, say feather please.
Caw, says crow, he will not speak.
Time for the hunting knife trick
I think, time for the grease and
the blade. Say feather crow, say
feather with a curved tongue, save
yourself. Caw says crow, caw once
before once after, the tear.
Who is there to hear whisper
of crow flown south tongue forked?
Feather is too soft for words,
feather is the sound of goose
flying south for the winter
carrying sky on her back.
Wait for me goose, whispers crow.

If you want to catch girl,

Slip of the Tongue III

If you want to catch girl first
find her sleeping, in a cave
or castle or garden she must be
asleep that's the rule. Now stoop
to her lips, stoopsuck the poison
from her finger the apple stuck
into her throat, the rule here
is to stoop. She will wake
in a flutter of eyes and lips,
her breasts if you care to look
will flutter also. She will say
where am i who are you i love you
she will draw you down to the catch
of her lips where her tongue winds,
I was going to say, like a snake
and kiss you long and lithe
unwind your soul on the pale
bobbin of her tongue, you will
fall asleep for a hundred years.

Last Fall

Late in the greengarden shadows
fatten, a girl peels her legs pale there
are crystals at her ears, wild facets
gather a last fall of light. It is
late tongue is weary tongue is

hungry.

I have cut my teeth on language, I am
tongue ticking with tricks and fraud
ticktock ticktock, tongue pendulum
of speech of silence, dingdong.

Night

the colour of windows blows
wide. Girl swings and spangles
her ears kite the stars, crystal falls
listen, somewhere, and falls. It is
late tongue leeches throat, sucks

mouth

bloodful as a tick. Tumerous I
divide as I eat igniting the wild
wild cells to fire in flesh, all the
slipped stitches unraveled in

me

in memory, of girl in greengarden
swinging the black hole of her belly. She
is dwarfstar now, see her devour suns
swallow moons core the world and her own
heart appled to a fall, picking teeth with

tongue.

The Ruby Garrote

this way to the barnum & bailey greatest show on earth this way to the barnum & bailey

    gaudy she stands on one leg
    on a painted horse the circus
    is language too   the power
    of faces, cumulative

    as irregular conjugations
    of acrobats small words sentenced
    to circle the ring letters flung
    through spotlight rosie knows

    correspondences   all metaphor
    nothing but trapeze weightless
    as the loss of flight the pitch
    & fling of consonants   she

    sleeps between the letters
    of the alphabet in white
    expanse of page come morning
    the men drive stakes into

    earth heave & sling against
    the wind against the rhetoric
    of gravity chronicle stretched
    to canvas between poles

ladies and gentlemen please welcome please welcome please welcome please

    petco the ringmaster stares at the world through the watchmaker's glass screwed into the socket of his hollow eye ticktock says the clock in his head that claps time with cupped hands after his last performance the ringmaster draws the flap swallows the key climbs into bed with cunning disdain afraid his chickenbones will crackackack since he survived that earthquake in far off agadir that killed off a townful think of that a townful now he doesn't want to tamper with what nature thought worth salvaging yes he wants to live forever ticktock says the clock no you won't i won't let you already sixty minutes less than an hour ago when i first started clapping out time like applause   if he knew what that time goblin knows he would stab it to death he would twist off its hands shatter its face petco the ringmaster's a clock-killer at heart would rather live without applause than not at all

never before in the history of the world never before in the history of the world

    rosie envies the stability of tables
    four legs to clamp the earth apart
    she has two, balances on one lost
    her head to a clown with a pigeon
    in his ear rosie is all centrifuge
    and line now headless she spins
    resinous flanks if she slows she un
    ravels her plume to the shaft if she
    stops the world falls from its horse

    i was the kid at the end of the street
    watching the circus strut through town
    i was the kid at the end of the stick
    tufting candyfloss to the wind
    it is mornings that horrify   days
    flip through a deck of cards the sun
    spun to beginning of sky here am i
    one foot five toes all of them broken
    to tread the turning world to roost

    rosie claims a conspiracy of circles
    quoit her round a minor galaxy she
    pivots her brass axis the horse gallops
    round and the ring and the tent and
    the world plunge through space clatter
    her waist catch at bright tulle
    a headless girl stands in a spotlight
    gathers all circles about her begins
    to twitch her hips begins to hulahoop

the clowns are dying all over the world the clowns are dying

                                    all over the world their faces
ajar luminous as dials under their wigs charred cogs
winch down never again will this story be told as if
it were the first one   wingspan of eyebrow to rout
the sky an uncivil joy of clowns leaked somewhere
between synapse a seizure of small wheels in the end
gaunt men spit in palms sweep from the ring a little
muddle of sawdust & zinc a smile split to fruit the
windfall of glance gone bad on the branch who cares
not i said the dead clown shucking skin whatever falls
out of my head falls into my pocket and reaches into
antique cage of rib to wind the clockwork bird that
squalls him carnal again blowing worlds like balloons
ardent and green

roll up and see and see and see roll up and see and see and see roll up and see

    rosie hunkers in her body
    whistles wind through flute
    of rib   love has strung her
    gravid at last run to earth
    she falls off her horse and

    into love with him the world
    spins on since the day damned
    if you didn't somersault right
    out of your shoes and back
    damned if you didn't wink

    the greenest eye now she's
    clunky with love one step
    and her cunt falls out a wedge
    of rusty iron on the ground if
    he doesn't love her back she

    will vanish from the plume from
    the posters the tent what's more
    my teeth will fall out oh what
    did you do do do to make me love
    you and why don't you love me

    too he sticks to her bones that
    man   as for me i am half-blown
    with love broken and the world
    so far away i think i can say
    this now i think i can say this

direct from the grasslands of the serengeti i give you beauty and her magnificent beast direct

the beast has found me out at last
looped in reverie of leaves breathes
heavy and almonds   sockets hairless
and rare all hollows laid bare
i swallow blood not mine

it is afterwards her hair blown
to the colours of tiger   eyes
slowburning the tilted world
somewhere the beast breathes
ripe and nut somewhere beast

grows hands

come one come all see the fattest woman in the world come one come all see the fattest

    going to have to let love
    eat you up says the fat lady
    ruminative to her man knitting
    skin the textures of carnival

    she throws a bone clicks
    her needles body seamed
    open to the gaze that
    yarns her yawns her she

    is opera all thaw and belly
    nights at circus hefting
    the carapace of his skull
    mandibles soft mumbling

    the mutinous folds sweet
    meat she thieves him some
    one should eat her all up
    someone should kiss her

**mesdames et monsieurs boys and girls voilà the marvelous marinelli
mesdames et monsieurs**

always announced in the dark
of the ring light falling, a face
delivered to grace at last one last
time they are so graphic the fallen

spangled to the precision
of rain sold his skeleton
to the devil they say
switchback he fakes it now

snakes it why he can move
quicker than thoughts of knife
twine gravity to the circlet
of his throat juggle planets

why he can play his ribs
for a harp pull pigeons & ribbon
from air and there is a trick
you can do with a girl and

a hat meanwhile knives rattle
their cages click to his bones he
slices a smile of venial teeth
straps me in body whistling

so eager his knives for the space
body gapes open, fingers thighs
nothing like death at the end
of a blade the ruby garrote, our body's

dark ore, he smiles a circle
of light so eager his teeth
for the soul's tender place so eager
my life by the grace of his knife

and now and now and now and now and now and now and now and now and

    let's us two clowns go halvsies   i have a nose a pair of shoes
a string of pearls that die if they're ignored a cat who'd scorn
to die because ignored a paintbox of delicious names a coat with
pockets that remembers things i've long forgotten coloured beads
and keys and halfsucked lemondrops and a pair of hands   you can
have half of everything if you let me share your treehouse the one
with green shutters that burnt down long ago the dog called *dog*
that died before you were born your five o'clock shadow that peaks
at four the matted sweater you climb into pull over your head in
stead of me a sense of direction that guidedogs you about cities
and my body with your eyes closed   oh   and your hands of course
knuckles chafed palms yellow with surfeit of butternut we'll swap
hands my right for your left or any other combination like prisoners
of war we will swap hands at dawn

whilst his lordship juggles top hat & cane her ladyship takes tea on the highwire whilst

    amongst her mirrors my lady
    stoops to placate a curl
    segmented and savoury
    she awaits her pleasure

    his lordship inserts
    a wedgewood spout
    pours himself into
    her bonechina interiors

    the best ceylon tea
    draws slowly emitting
    only an elegant wisp
    of steam at regal intervals

    reappareled she
    adjusts an eyebrow
    walks out briskly
    to be seen to take

    the air there
    goes my lady stropped
    and streetwise
    gurgling with hot tea

four lions two tigers two black bears two polar bears four

    lions trained but not tamed
    two wild tigers recently captured
    two black bears two white bears
    a man with a whip   this
    paix dans la jungle a tale

    of apples and figleaves
    of shame forgotten at last the lost
    hierarchy of animals and angels
    when the earth flew wings and
    hooves pale quattrocento

    light breaking through look
    a lion rampant on a shield
    two bears rearing crimson
    & chivalric the protocol
    of unicorns   their archaic

    despair beyond light spectators
    rattle their cages snicker
    grunt   feeding time at the zoo
    again the subtle relish of beef
    a humid infection   the ardent

    flesh turning meat on slow
    rotisserie of eye obscenity
    of tooth and claw in human
    hair and someone always tasting
    blood at the back of the throat

The Fallen Here

Fairytales from the Old Country

Long ago as the crow flies there was a man who invented ships
in bottles with meticulous fingers and a fine alkaline mind and
a pair of sterling silver tweezers as long as his patience
was long for everyone but a clumsy son   the kind of boy who
couldn't quite tie his laces balancing on one foot couldn't
quite catch a ball a girl a bus a joke was always chosen second
to last on football teams shamed his father with sweatypalmed
love when he tried to help he tried to help one day and sank
a fleet of frail ships at sea in their jaunty bottles allatonce
glass everywhere heart-struck glass in its rigging of chest (a
sneaking joy surges at the bloodtides in sight of that
glorious anarchy) broken bottlenecks crushed hulls frayed rope
abandon ship   his father that digital man took one litmus look
and beat his son silly taking care in his fine ship captain's
fury that the blows were confined to the hands of that clumsy
troublesome unlovely loveless boy I never wanted you he raged I
never wanted you   he hit him only on the hands even his anger
precise   the hands of the boy swelled in the night turned
blue by morning the skin was tight with blood tight with blood
and dark with the smell of it and death   sweet jesus said
the surgeon these'll have to come off the father killed himself
with a single shot in the middle of the forehead left his son
stretching out white stumps crying i did it daddy i did it i'm
sorry promise i won't daddy please daddypleasedaddyplease
daddy give me back my hands   once there was a man who loved

rain and stones cradled small things in the eggcups of his palms
one hot summer night when breathing was like taking ether he
fell asleep and dreamed tarantulas climb to the sunken darkness
of his mouth trail web from his dusty navel (thump)   went his
heart something (thump went his)   landed on his *thump* without
the consolation of indecision without thought he tears small
bones apart with raw hands then sleeps starting awake with the
pewtered dawn outside the window broken on flagstone smudge
of grey kitten leaks to death   once upon a time a fond uncle
stooped to greet his favourite niece hallo my darling he swung
her into the air by the neck hallo my darling until she died
what have you done cried her mother snatching her dead darling
from his gentle hands   only this he says lifting the other
child hands on either side of her round child's neck depressing
as the doctor would tell them later the carotid artery that
pulses at the source of the throat only one in ten million have
a weakness there but for those   he coughs bleakly   death is
inevitable   b b but i only d d did this the fond uncle cries
hands trembling like turned leaves he demonstrates lifting her
little sister by the neck to the sky until she dies hanging
from her gentle murderer's hands the chances of that happening
twice in one family exclaims the doctor carried away from grief
by statistics   is incredible once   a boy lost his hands and
his father two girls and a kitten their lives once.

Any Old Skin

I never saw a snake before I saw the first snake I ever saw
a pulsing red muscle on the path throbbing with the noonsun
in a green saladbowl of a country odiferous with chicory
and vinegar. I never ran so fast as on that day sluggish blood
whisked suddenly through dark corridors rung in the high
chambers of ears pulled at the slow clapper of a heart brassy
with fear and genesis. I swear it wasn't the old myths that did
for me I hardly thought of sin that day I thought of the old man
who leered at me pulled down his pants to flash me a handful
of red muscle. I laughed afterwards and told them all of the sad
old man thought he would shock a grown woman with his eyes
half cocked and his threebagshalf full I never told them
of the snake though and the silence that followed the whole
valley writhing in coils with that length of looped rope
slung casually on the path the sun gone dark as venom.

Fooling the Jasmine

The way we creak out of winter
into the hurting season
green buds winched from bone
an early thaw every afternoon
in this city the scent of
jasmine every afternoon
in this city.

Her nails the colour
of consumption, she no longer
paints. We go beyond art
you see, here we do not trust
ourselves to live why I
can't even tell him I love him
et j'ai lu tous les livres.

Next season I will plant jasmine
on that wall and bougainvillaea
he says. In the ten years of prison
he did not lose faith, shaved
every day. What did you learn
he was asked afterward. In trees
a twist of pigeons open to paper.

                       In this city
jasmine every afternoon
in this city the scent of
an early thaw every afternoon
green buds winched from bone
into the hurting season
the way we creak into winter.

The Fallen Here

Come to the edge
No we will fall
Come to the edge
No we will fall
Come to the edge
He pushed them and they flew
                    Guillaume Apollinaire

This story of a homecoming
five lemons sizzle in a blue bowl
at the roadside. The sun
squeezed us sour you thought
of whitebait the pucker
of rice carried them home
in twist of newspaper they hissed
in the dark squeezed dry
with the sun in chipped enamel
of sky. The places
we have been happy
hold up such empty hands
after absence you can fall in love
with buildings too everything
is glass now you keep meeting
yourself wherever you go even
the cactus strains to gaze
like a woman in the oval droop
of her looking glass. This
is a country where women of a certain
age still totter through the noonhour
in pale dresses and high ideals
propriety propriety. For years now
you have talked in the past tense
about yourself *come to the edge he said*
no we will fall. A woman falls
in the street you reach to help
she flinches mistrust rheuming

her eyes and her stockings also
are torn, we do not touch the fallen
here.
                    Sebokeng
is looking for an apartment in the city
come on up said the landlady when
he rang then she saw him oh. So
many meetings swarm through this one
when you left that time you left
he said I watched you get into the plane
it was like a coffin sliding into earth.
Come to the edge (we will fall we will)
that summer was too hot for the quilt
you slept under like a lover. We thought
they were stupid said Brother Giovanni
we had no idea they were hungry. A man
on the corner holds up his sign, please
god to help me no food for three days.

Money changes hands the lights change
colour and cars move on. How long
will it take? From the beginning
to the end, you must spend
your life returning he said.

Such a Long Way

                    Love now,
a kind of homesickness.

How does it smell, a whiff
of paraffin, how does it sound,
it has no sound, how does it
taste? Like pennies on the tongue

if grief is not too strong a word
for fugitive loss, a kind of haunting.
Flicker of cat in the shadows long after
she had died, the first time I mean.

All animals find a home or die.

Sometimes she surprises herself with homes
she has claimed, the word *bicycle*
smell of jasmine, her mother's pots, there
is more there is more, cool lip
of a fluted white cup, this
is Illyria, lady. Writing
the opposite of home, every letter
a window: dear everyone
here is a list of things that come back:

        pigeons
        frisbees
        astronauts
        palindromes
        the moon
        true north
        your hands

Somewhere in the world it is spring, a surplus
at the border, a season not earned. Look
for me in the damp crevices of summer, I
have beaten out my time in gold paint and tin.

String Quartet

Prima parte moderato

This is not about music this is about desire. The desire that rides us, four horses on a carousel. When the music stops we are obliged to change horses. How did I, the first violin, learn of desire this temperate man this musician of controlled vibrato and perfectly creased trousers? There was a spot on her hand, it preoccupied her immensely. She rubbed at it, a cat with buttered paws.

So little it takes.

If I were of a poetic tone of mind I would say she holds her viola to her chin as if it were a head. A beloved mortal head aah the degeneracy of that mouth composting kisses. She is rotten as camembert I tell you.
Also she is holding her bow too high again and slicing.
Slicing. Tonight I will tell her of the moderate elbow that pivots in its ballbearings. No more slicing I will whisper in the secret of her ear. And I will slice her open like a letter yes. And she will be all paper and flutter at my feet ... *moderato moderato.*

Seconda parte allegro

why always the long wet slant what am i *donnina allegra* a loose woman?
always with him the gaze brimming over eyes swimming little fishes in
brine surely she sees him her husband watches him watching me

watching her

she is so distant tonight the reflection of a woman caught in the
mirror who was it said beauty is measured in the distance between eyes
the length of the nose her neck is too long the sad nun's throat of a
modigliani nude a bowl of lemons in the foreground someone should kiss
her all over bite that hard red berry make her moan i would like to
hear her moan see those flat eyes fly open watch the palms for stigmata
i would like to make her moan does he make her does he there is blood
moving below the surface of her wrist sometimes in my sleep i see that
pale drowned face hanging over his shoulder like a scarf as he ramps
and plunges her eyes fathom green and salt sink to the bottom of sea
she takes me between her thighs plays me like a cello

Recapitulazione della prima parte moderato

Moderato moderato ... and she will be all paper and flutter at my feet. And I will slice her open like a letter yes. No more slicing I will whisper in the secret of her ear. Tonight I will tell her of the moderate elbow that pivots in its ballbearings. Slicing. Also she is holding her bow too high again and slicing. She is rotten as camembert I tell you. A beloved mortal head aah the degeneracy of that mouth composting kisses. If I were of a poetic tone of mind I would say she holds her viola to her chin as if it were a head.

So little it takes.

She rubbed at it a cat with buttered paws. There was a spot on her hand it preoccupied her immensely. How did I, the second violin, learn of desire this temperate man this musician of controlled vibrato and perfectly creased trousers? When the music stops we are obliged to change horses. The desire that rides us, four horses on a carousel. This is not about desire this is about music.

Coda legato molto

What the first violin loves the second violin tries to love. What the first violin desires the second violin is obliged to desire so it goes so it goes. What an excursion into the grotesque what a parody this is and I quite aloof from it all, angular and undismayed. Tonight as always he will blunder to her door I will hear the bedsprings and his sprung cries, a fugue of desire. Then I will smooth out his trousers and lay them flat on the board and iron and iron the creases to darts.

What goes around goes around.

And of course he hears them too, the second violinist, their aleotoric grindings. And I wonder for whom he throbs at these times, for him or her, the object of his desire or the object of his desire's desire? As for me I have long ceased to throb I am all calloused fingers now suppleness of wrist is all.

Round and round.

Thing is, the music changes every night the horses dance up and down up and down who knows where I'll be next time round. Perhaps then, the next time this body this cello will be tuned *con molto affetto*

with love.

Days of Water

Start perhaps with the waters
broken she and her three
sisters just for the pleasure
of looking, cut surface

light winces the long
long wick of gaze, the glare
so this is the world she said,
the first sister turned tail.

Or start, with headlong
calamity of sky, a gull
shuddering feathers. As above
so below, said the second

goodbye. Sea and sky hinge
open. Dingdong said the third,
was gone. The engulfed
city chimes turret & tower

strikes clearlight, rings stone
highpitched as bell. Beginagain:
cutting water a cleanrun
the minnowed sea the sun

drawing her poison.

∾

Just for the pleasure of looking just
for the pleasure of looking just for
the pleasure of looking just for the
pleasure of looking just for the pleasure

then she saw him and turned salt.

∾

So this is the world, thrashing
through days of water, wiring
gone subtly awry someone
has salted her tail she

sheds in scales somewhere
a fish slips the mesh the net
unthreads that soft palate
blood wells her mouth bitter

as placenta. The world rolls
over slaps wet thighs
she closes her eyes hatches
the moondeep in her belly.

∾

What can write asked the seawitch
her truant mother, but cannot read?
Your footprints in the sand. Pared
to cuticle she sprawls rock

the space between her thighs
gives way seeks its own sealevel
in her belly's wild sargasso
caverns amniotic & brine.

There was a shark said the seawitch
her truant mother, there was a knife
I cut his tongue until it bled
ate himself up from the inside

out. This is the way to kill the fish
the hunger that marauds in circles
also the story of language. They say
each step was like walking on knives

balanced on blade of heel
tracking webfeet across sand
to stand at his feet. What beauty
is this he cries her tongue flaps wide

somewhere bird surfaces, a rag
of fish in beak. She squawks once
antics the world to particle
and noise. He is teaching her

to speak. Say love he says, say
light say heart say rain. *Rain*,
language slices her tongue
to flounder, never again that hunger.

∽

In the dear harbour of his arms
fingering slow keel of spine bent
to her lit waters, ruddering
the floor threequarter

time. Anemones
open and close in her eyes.
The pucker of seaweed
her hair a deep trawl

gathering him in slick
through galaxies of mirror perhaps
he will drown in her hair perhaps
she will drown in the air.

The ballroom tilts off axis
into counterfeit and night
there is a temptation here
to speak of stars the moon,

say stars clung to their feet
like rosin, a halfmoon misshapen

as desire. And day, soundless
as the colour of water in three

quarter time. The measure
of waltz is feet the beat
of pulse at wrist, beneath
dovetail of ankle, each step

like knives.

∾

and then he kissed me
my heart went thunk but my
bones rang clear he said
i have been asleep these

hundred years my body
empty and hooded a bell
my mouth tastes the brass
i am ready i think for

a finetuned tongue the wet
shriekiek of teeth on glass
this is the moment before
analogy a moment later

the kiss like water

∾

Blunt thumbs fumble
at her split seams
pick unpick her
from the warp of sleep
thumbed open

dogeared she awakes
gloss of shears
poised like a body
over her body. Bone
and brainless she

traded a tail for legs
gained the space
between them still
slipstitched shut he
will cut smartly

against the bias.
When laid on her back
her eyes close gently it
never fails, there
is a spring you see

at the base of neck
her lips part when
her legs do. She can
sing through her nose
wriggle her ovaries

swallow her own saliva
and his and say
ohyesohyesohyesoh
and when
it's all ohohoh–over

and out thighs drawn
in a catscradle of wet
cotton why she will
stitch it closed again she
can do that too.

∾

He will never love you said her mother
if you were cinnamon on the tongue

soon he will say your thighs open
him to fields of strawberry inhaling

all in a ferment of drawn breath
the strawberry is a fruit of no aftertaste

no regret. Afterwards when he brailles
your spine blindfingering each slow

bone tell yourself you are the abacus
on which his beads are strung each

one slotted into place even the space
between notched pliant and willow.

He never loved me said her mother
though he pressed his ear to my green

navel and turned his sailor's
tongue into mollusk

frothed salt in the convolutions
of shell pried my small

mouthful of pearl down his
throat infected me with the hard

ardour of sailors spawned
me upstream to spin

in salmonthrashed water. He will
never love you said her mother.

∾

This is how it ends, he pastes
a kiss like a postage stamp on
her eyelid leaves without once
looking back looks back

(turns stone). Drops a note
by the time you read this

winches palms long
& lotus round her throat, moults

in feathers at her feet, tracks
a dusty message: *there
is no life after this ornamental
death.* His kiss turns crow he'll

throw a handful of knuckle
in her lap as he leaves he leaves
no forwarding address only his pale
ribcage fanned at her

feet. The kiss spoils on her lips
a rose junking petals he slits
to the hilt pares the rind
of skin turned hieroglyph

translates her body
into all the dead & beautiful
languages before they turn
to ash. Girl hangs in sky

upside down goodbye goodbye.

∞

These things then were grooved
the edges of the sea the earth

blacklipped gaping for seed
the bark of cedar the bite

of teeth against applecore
the sound fish make whistling

through water the washingboard
hair of angels also feathers

walnuts corduroy the flutes
of mushrooms the diphthongs

of the old language the mother
tongue also wings and flies, a lie.

These things were grooved
the ridges of your nails the roof

of your mouth.

∞

For Breath & Glass

All Day

Today we read this city mapped
beneath wet fingers thumb her
open, fumble each fervent stone.
I will start with the colours there is
no colour for morning for the duration
of light moving on an open door. No
colour for the sour longing of a sax
a sudden transparency of hour, hours
blown one by one
the negligence of wine glasses.

You can buy wine by the glass here also
water by the hour. All day we open
this city in sections on our laps while
rain rubs light to pewter & lamp.
Along these streets walked Dante Alighieri
says the guidebook turning its own
pages in excitement.
All these years with only the rain between.
What we are searching for: a sudden white
intensity of thought thin as paper.

If I say I know you now, it is only
in my error. Error of feet, the glottal click
of stone on bone.
Along these streets we saw an old man
on a bicycle, his shoulderblades opened

closed like wings. Somewhere in the old city
an imprint of thumb   I will say
one more thing before I leave: that rain
this oblique city, doubles the world

or halves it, as you would say
folding me carefully down the spine.
This is the way stairs pull you up
their slope, throw you open to birds
cursive in the decline of sky (last
night was as long as a candle)
I would like to say bodies open
like maps, invoke the assonance
of wax and tongue, slow turnings
behind deep shutters.

When you open a door in a street

When you open a door in a street in Milan
there is the possibility of colours dazed & blood
a virgin's slow burning
and figures kneeling in sudden *chiaroscuro*.

In passing a courtyard in Milan, an ivory
rattle of satin, the hoarseness of wedding cloth
billowing behind wrought iron. Venus
touches herself slyly between weeded thighs.

Walking home past the windows of Milan
night falls in another language, lovers
hold their bodies to the light heavy
with sediment.

I will tell you something now my love
that home is always somewhere
else, the world is haunted by windows,
the jubilance of doors announce us.

On your left above the fireplace
you can see the gothic arch where
the infamous Council of 10 sat that
is the lion's mouth where citizens
posted their accusations.

    Here in Venice we are obsessed
    with perspective, the world stirring
    always at the corners of our eyes.
    Mornings flexing into bridge
    a frail intimacy of umbrella
    the smallest arch to live inside.

This is the ante-chamber and that
is the torture chamber notice the
thumbrack in the glass case please
do not touch do not take photographs
descend the stairs and keep together.

    It is noon the merchants
    take down their awnings. Behind shutters
    women peel fruit, touch themselves.
    In cafés we move awkwardly in light
    beyond filament and immolation
    and the truancy of wings.

If you turn your head at the window
you will catch the last sight of Venice
glimpsed by the condemned from this
Bridge called Sighs as you can see
the light is appalling.

      We grow old here quickly
      water, our disease & festivity.
      There are so many disguises
      it is no longer possible to die.
      Inside the masks at carnival
      our faces inert as clocks.

Toward a Catalogue of Falling

                This is what endures
a ridge of teeth a lyric
column stuttering in broken sunlight
the doric rhyme of stone
and sky. Vesuvius brought tragedy

to Pompeii it proved the city's fortune
a guide instructs his group *you are*
sightseers in a dead city. We enter
by the sea gate through architecture
of particle and air. Say nothing

there is ash on my tongue, words
turned fossil against the lining
of mouth. We read graffiti
off the public walls, reminders of debts
money received, declarations of love

obscenities. Now in this ringing
blue space in this uplift of stone
turn to me with empty palms
and conjugate past lives
I fell I fall I have fallen.

Who ran fastest on that day who
stayed behind to help the old?
Pliny the younger tells how day
fell backwards into night, another fall.
I am the storyteller of me

there is nothing to tell, we know
little of Pliny, his fall from grace.
The tourists are listening to their guides
in five languages they hold umbrellas
cameras, listen to the rain how it

falls. So this is what endures
broken columns of spine, of stone, a verb
inventory of all falling, the fallen
lucid girls in their hair (they say
you die before you hit rock still

I am not dead yet.) The tourists dredge
bread into olive oil, take pictures, the light
was birdless slanting from the sky broken
open on raw stone. Beggars gather, *english
guide very good very little money* do not

fall for it.   Aah love
there is nothing you can tell that
will satisfy what I want
to know of you, of me
there is nothing to tell. As for Vesuvius

I never saw such languor *let us hope*
her sleep lasts a thousand years the last
ride home on the *circumvenicular*, the children
crying, the young men in the imperative mood
failed to wake her, fallen with the lapsed century

asleep.

Vertical cities

slide off their mountains and into the sea
creak gaunt eaves to the wind
bend bend like the cypress, and break
and broken learn again to bend.

No virtue in this shattered stone, it's how
the light gets out. Hoarded in crook
of root, oleander and the tree
that bursts into a seasonal apostrophe

of lemons. Cities that kindle the past to flame
& forgiveness, never once look back never
stare at that greeneyed sea, listen
that is not your name on the wind that

is not my voice. Your mouth
in this altitude
an oil press. Noon slumps
through foliage and flesh

no longer at ease with faith or gravity
we grow used to legs swung over time
eat grapes from the vine, spit seed we
turn footless with the tide.

Some Place

In the memory of a leavetaking
it is raining through the reticence
of black and white film. There

are angels who commute by train
whistling through their teeth, wings
folded into string baskets. A woman

sits with her parcels between
her legs, thinks *the light from stars
requires time*, watches her face

slip mackerel through canals
considers other lives. Can't remember
now why I wanted to come to Bologna

a name slid open in my throat
I caught a train. Some faces
cannot be translated, some hands

do not speak english. Some place
never travelled I have prepared
all my life to accomplish.

Epigrams for Breath & Glass

three clocks along victor emmanuelle

three different times the fourth holds up empty
hands in the night all clocks in the city turn
back one hour   we wake up ahead of ourselves

today is the sixth

according to *il tempo* somewhere a day
has been lost   I turn out my pockets
nulla, this is just to say wish you were

someone always being kissed

on a bridge in this city last night when
the gypsies came to town flying candles a flutter
of cards I want to have my palm read in italian

michelangelo's bound slaves try to free themselves

he knew something of bondage, the incurable mortar
quarried from bone I know more: no festive revolt
out but in, a dissolution through sonnet to stone

the women who smell like

out of season freesias when you lift them from
paper spills, unchill in heated rooms
white lilies in the place of their grief

and then in siena

the old man his jacket slung on the wire hanger
of shoulderblades framed by an arch and lifting
with weary elegance a cigarette, his ruinous mouth

in the rain yesterday a man

walked towards me cradling the day's sadness beneath
his umbrella and the woman on the train today writing
a letter in blue ink how do you spell *carmine* she asks

what can I say of the island

shall I speak of the marquetry of light the slow stretch
of beach a horizon somewhere out of reach? the grand hotel
was closed for restoration, service entrance to your left

what I want to say, after naples

after the long wait for the ferry, sour trough
of sea, after the sudden displacement to land
a draught cool & bottomless, a month of birds

vinçenzo has a beard

seeded with salt   and eva was beautiful
when she was young vinçenzo sculpted her she
has the tender columella of the forgetful

{ # Elsewhere
}

Light, moving

You had forgotten that words can be replaced, to begin
again is a point of honour. Like the beginning
of reading, how you spread honey on a page, as sweet
as this honey, so is learning. In the split light of noon
this city does not forgive us our trespasses.
Above the Alfama, the streets a contagion of light
and the opposite of light, somewhere the click of anklebone
on cobble.

This afternoon when we sat on the rim of the old city
sharing a pair of binoculars, a man many miles away
adjusted with terrible intimacy, his tv aerial.
During siesta, an hour opaque as forgiveness, all
water in the city pauses, resumes asynchronous.
I stop myself before I write, *houses fall like dice
toward a sea as blue as a synonym* (I was raised
a cubist, with a sense of astonishment) and bougainvillaea
caught *in flagrante delicto*. It is the beginning of the month
when gravity is strongest, climbing out of bed today
she stumbled but did not fall. In this heat our fingers
fatten subtly in the night so that rings
are awkward, mnemonic.

All day they watch tourists blot sun against thin skin
her shutter clicking amiably across the film she had forgotten
to replace, anticipating always the moment that precedes them
when they spill, glossy squares of colour from an envelope

slit by a wet forefinger. And Lisbon now,
smelt of green leather and diesel, the sour pout of dust
at the back of the throat. Wine, sharp olives, this day together
after an absence of years, the water, even the bread
salty with defections.

This is the sentence you write before you fall asleep
in the book that will later be lost somewhere between Madrid
and El Escorial: *only the animals defer to these curt*
afternoons, dogs lie where they fall in the squares
cats divide themselves from their shadows, and sleep
through siesta that lasts from the time it takes for light
to move across an open doorway, from left
to right, reading.

Worn Through

On the southwest corner of this continent, at Sagres, her father
walks out behind thrifty scrub to photograph a sea that she
has for three days now resisted as colour, what
is still not possible to say?

His hands that look like a child's drawing of hands,
the colour of sea, the photograph that will never be developed
(they do not know this yet): these things
cannot be grasped except in effigy.

Elsewhere is the direction in which the fishermen along
the seawall gaze.

At Cascais we bought figs and split them against
the backs of our thumbs. The city was worn through,
a penny in the lining of a careless pocket.
In this summer residence of sultans, old men
eyes closed against lineage and the sun who
pretending to fall asleep, fall asleep. In the bottled
warmth of the car she knows enough now
not to ask her mother a direct question.

On the drive home they pass almond, olive groves
poisonous oleander, trees corkscrewed in the dust,
the sweet hum of spanish broom and in the middle
distance, at the moment when the horizon unlatches,
the lilac urgency of furze.

Later, after the droop of sunflowers in the west
after the postcard signed with a row of authentic
blue kisses, after the candle gutted in spilt wine:
this wild page postponed in the absence of
a witness. She is remembering the moment in the car
before they saw him rounding a curve of sky, when
they imagined he had abandoned them momentarily
but forever, at the edge of this bitter
coffee-scented continent.

Various Blues

Amongst cork trees, Evora, medieval and gnomic after a long drive
on bad roads. We woke early, made sandwiches with goat's-milk
cheese and sardines, tomatoes, very red. There is
a temptation here to read metaphorically, to record that she
scribbled furiously on her white cuffs a group of words
superior to any sentence. We parked beneath the city walls
but the road passed through us and on into the interior,
here even time has a crease down the centre.

This story follows its own dirt tracks, we entered
in their wake through improbable streets
ate hot chestnuts in the rain, a corrupt palate.
At the *universidade*, Maria studies english, portuguese
talks mostly with her hands. Her stockings a scandal
of inexact seams, I have seen her look better
but never more ingenious. *In its desire to be loved
this city opens itself to us like a map, produces
the truths we require.*

We climb to the perspective of trees, jacaranda
sings various blues strident in the spaces between
key changes. The cathedral through a sudden crook of leaf
startles itself into abrupt jigsaw, reassembles.

Unlike the scent of lemon that escapes stone, to repeat
itself approximately on the wind.

A street begins beneath the hooves of a cart-horse
ends in a detour that can only be satisfied elsewhere.
When I get home I will begin a journal of coincidences
starting with the synchronicity of architecture and bone.
In this heat, Maria says, *I am disinclined to wear colours
not replicated in nature.* I think: brick, umber, stone,
tongue.

The word *nature* used here without malice, as in, women
who appreciate nature only by way of a 4 x 6 glossy.

Inside this church, perverse and rapturous, *Capela de Ossos,
we bones lie here awaiting yours.* Five hundred *escudos*
extra to take a photo, the ticketseller festive in the last
hour of her working day. Inside, the word *bone*, blunt
shaft of light across the temple. Outside
the rain, x-ray of bright bone against the sky.

Into Category

Doors in this latitude mark time, an angular crop
between light and its transgressions. Contrary to history
that begins with the past, a genealogy begins with this
present generation, rectangles of light blazing sideways
in an abrupt noon. At Loulé, a market town, she watches,
for some time, a woman slice eels along the chronology
of spine. Her knife silver, I could say, mute.
Across counters, tangle of chainmail and gilt rings
scale like spare change. What I have deleted
from this sentence were her raw palms turning from flesh
into category like the arms of the woman this morning
who left her balcony the moment before the camera clicked.
A visual fallacy, she has already lived through
all possible exposures in the world.

Her vehement, careless arms.

One could say the doorway forces us to read
laterally, across surface. Still, something charming
in the way doors resist their own pleasure, close flush
refuse to gape, even in our extremest hour. We
climb to Alte, a possibility coarse with salt of dried cod.
This was the place we resisted at first, a little scar
in small letters on an open map.

In photographs, she looks so like her mother, you'd think
they were related. But the town was charming and disgruntled,
along thresholds, dogs weary in the anticipation of a season
shrugged. And the men playing boule, each word a mouthful
of pale green wine.

Later, the artisan helps her from the floor of his studio
that smells of citrus, hot skin, wipes against his shirt
the dust from her hands, goodbye. This town
does not look back, salty into the imperfect past
and the fat geranium she picked, wilted
on the windshield for days. This,
the garden we touched once then forgot, a transparent
language lucid as a glass jar filled to the brim
with water. The shadow on the wall, her only alibi
I was here, girl with windy hair.
That night she unfolds his inky name, mouths
it once before she falls asleep to swing all night
on the unlatched door that requires, like writing,
a witness.

Water, falling

The road to Granada is copperplate, a rise and fall
of Andalusian cursive. She fell asleep after that sentence
woke to find herself slant amongst hills, the air
precipitate with spanish broom, a gradient of trees sudden
as windmills. Two hundred years ago, the sky's
wild summer skin and trees reckless against walls.

We work through the Alhambra according to Michelin, watch a guide
lead her group into the notorious Galeria de Abencerrajes where
the sultan piled the heads of the sons of his first wife. *Notice
the sophistication of the drainage, how the blood could depart
by way of the gutter.* In her wake such delirium
of goldleaf & candle drafting light to slake a thirst
past bearing, long past. Who can catch the invisible
sing the unnameable? A soul, snatched up and spun
through cupola and mosaic, turns wax.

Tabacaria, papelaria, she takes pictures in italics, between
balconies dreaming iron, a casement chews geranium,
mumbling away. What the arches repeat to themselves
against bright curves of wall: oh yes oh yes oh yes oh –

The predominance in this town of arches provide a frame
for our inventiveness. In the stones of the *medina*, a snake
scribbles palindromes, and the man painted on the beerlabel
at Bodega Santa Cruz, holds up a painted bottle of beer.
It would not be untrue to say we found a rose

in the sultan's garden, colour of thick vellum
in a book with uncut pages. Because of the glare
reflected off walls, I am obliged to set my aperture
at 500th of a second.

In photographs her father holds her mother, including her
she would like to say, beneath the arch of his shoulder.

The way water is conserved, flows and drains. A woman
in the bodega lifts the glass stem of her throat, a long
pause at the bottom of the day. Or: the arch as hyphen,
a conjunction of the continuous present. Would be inaccurate
to say the river reflects the bridge, say rather the bridge
at the moment of the imperfect future, tensed and sprung. If
you are crafty with the shutter speed you may be lucky enough
to catch water, falling.

The cathedral from the middle distance: a narrow blade
of stone, colour of amnesia. It should be plain by now
that we are receding, traveling away from, glancing
back.

On whitewashed walls the lime trees sign their names.

Reading Oranges

Three things happened this afternoon in Malaga. A bus conductor
on the *ciudad real* called the wrong exit at carrera Santa Maria.
A woman buying a pair of silver earrings had them wrapped
in tissue paper as if they were flowers, out
of season. A man stopped suddenly beneath the window
of the school of flamenco in the old quarter.

My darling, this city is beautiful but I miss (I could say
a woman chooses fruit from straw baskets. A woman
in a photograph chooses fruit. She wears jeans,
a delicate nape shows vee through dark wings. Between
the anticipation of cilantro and flesh green as papaya
she hesitates forever. The word *urn* springs to mind here,
a consummation devoutly to be wished) I think
of your mouth as an antidote.

These things this afternoon in Malaga. The emphatic
smell of oilpaint confused for a moment the tourists
in the rooms of the Picasso museum. A woman selling
birdcages was caught momentarily in a complicated
passion of wicker. On the steps of the Plaza Obispo
before the statue of the virgin, a man kneels
startled by the plausibilities she offers.

Of course this is all speculation, a distraction of interiors
hasty with steam and spilt beer. A man hurries across
the street to buy matches, buys matches. Elsewhere
summer thickens along window ledges. In another country
you are awake, a small flower from the embroidered pillow
pressed into your cheek. Perhaps
I should tell you the nectarine I ate while sitting on the wall
tasted like the lining of your mouth. Both hold out to me
the extreme possibility of faithfulness in a broken world.

Three things before you go: the saint behind the avenue
of the artisans is reading oranges again with his fingers. At
the little cathedral of the lady with one arm, an old woman
smells cyclamen, *de nada*. In the english bookstore
the clerk searches recklessly for a translation of Lorca
mumbles *verde que te quiero verde*. Not one of these things
is an allusion to you.

On the plaza a woman in a linen shirt colour
of steamed milk is writing a postcard: *after all this
is not a love letter. I am free to speak of the grass along
Paseo del Parque held down by dandelions tender as buttons.*

Following Herself

Rolling a cigar casually down the length of a cool brown thigh.
We looked for you, Carmen, all over this city, intrigue and odd
banalities. A landscape arranges itself in her viewfinder.
Of four windows only one is open. A handswidth, the erotic
distraction.

Two days after the patio festival, the street of flowers still
cannot be paraphrased. Over this city, all its cautious patrons,
someone has poured a layer of apricot glaze, across tile across
cheekbones, a careful damascene. In her pocket a postcard,
even history, remember, had a referent once.

These lovesick streets teach us something of perspective
how they tug at the spur of our heels. At noon
the shadow is a woman following herself
past a shop called *Sirene*. Later she will sit
at a café, write, *I do not think I can traverse this city again
I will look for you elsewhere.* Behind her head, wicker
explodes, the invective of fruit, we are arrested by an authentic
corner of torn plaster, the original brick showing through.
I have waited at the place from which one stands to take
photographs, all this time, waited.

Triptych

Rumours of Bear

I

Rumours of bear in this lapsed valley
of uninflected pine, the lucid stones
cut slant. Somewhere in the forest
axe rings light the colours of iron
nobody has seen the bear seen the way
a spill of bark and cone uncurls
clatter of loose claws in a pocket
of gravel and night moving migrant
between restless paws. Only the eyes
strung to bead, caught avid
in crossfire. There is a rumour
slouching east along the highway
a bear is on the loose
fresh scat in the shape of snout
a woman gnawed tongueless, some
lost creature pacing out its salvation
in clumsy spoor follows its own milled
breath to the city, meets itself halfway.

11

Word of bear long before bear.
Fans stirred air to soup, fat
gusts of leather and saddle and
jerky on rope. Outside gas boiled
in canisters a woman awoke, tail
of dream still wet in her throat
there are mountains at the window
let them in let them in. Something
sunless and mendicant is gnawing
its paws, this was the day bear
came to town the sky fell blue into
the room. How do you enter a room?
At the door like a thief, down the chimney
like a gift, how do you enter
a room?

III

Through the window like the sky
bear comes snuffling the odour
of honey and onions gathered in
hair, her mineral blood truffles him
past earthworm and loam and finger
bones that click in the spaces
between streetlamps. Far away
a forest stands ajar, interlinear
of stride & desire. The dark arterial
paraphrase, his secret cartography.
Why even the crows know they are only
symbols in the heraldic slaying
of bear on field of argent, the colours
of his dying oilcloth and tapestry.
There should have been castles
and pennants and knights, there should
have been a virgin with hands like
bandages to close his wounds his eyes.

Like Rain

                The landscape
does not vindicate our likeness
five figures poise gingerly
on the edge of water.
Or take the word *mouth*
round as a vowel.

So I have come to this place
from so far away, a green parabola
fine rain sieved through skin
it is no longer possible to write
love poems or say *here I am*, here
at the day's
damp hinge, say it say
mouth.

A hundred words for green
in this damp language, enunciation
of tendril & leaf, here
at the dull syntax of rock
and throat, nothing to recall
the dead unless memory grows
purple and emphatic, splits rock.

As for the deer that crossed
our path that day the road
going on without us, they have already
passed out of the present tense. I saw
two deer she says (all day rain falls
like rain) falls here and here

this is a love poem perhaps the last one
I will ever write because of this business
with deer, words turned fossil
in the lining of mouth before we can
say flicker.

Woke up this morning, imprint
of hoof on her cheek.

Bestiary in Three Parts

And you in your high stony place, old woman
turning on the cusp of night, the borrowed
light of moons reveals you, a lateral section
glint & quartz against the grain, those were pearls
were pearls. Every year
at this time blood overflows its banks
the body reclaimed, perennial. Teach us to breathe
on an updraft, suck marrow from forgiveness, sprout
feathers in the throat, teach us to trace words
in the sky at our leaving, *garnet* and *rheumatism*.

Aslant their bittergreen eggs, hatching liver,
geese muse on the letter vee. Obsessed
with formation, the forethought of beak, the beginning
of vanity. How love pivots on the dead letter, the migratory
verb. A jewel sunk
to an access of appetite, who has known
such hunger? Already they have exhausted
all lexicon, what is left? An approximate
desire, the silences in eiderdown, a sky
closing slowly overhead.

An old woman looks upward, thinks of flying
south for the winter, to live again in the bright florals
of the weaned tongue where the sky, unfallen, is empty
as the mind of a pig dreaming tripe. Here
the world falters on equation, three quarters sky
wax slate of our unrepresentable longing. Perhaps she thinks
of the skeleton season, the tungsten gnaw
of dawn. This is, has always been, our only
home. Weary of analogy she remembers the old appetites
a monthly voluptuary of blood, the astringent palate.

Acknowledgments

Poems have previously been published in the following magazines and anthologies, my thanks to the editors: *Border Crossings, Contemporary Verse 2, The Fiddlehead, The Malahat Review, Poetry Canada, Prairie Fire, Prism International, Quarry, Qwerty, Vintage '93, Vintage '94, West Coast Line, Windhorse Reader.*

- *The Ruby Garrote* was published as a disOrientations chapbook, designed by Nicole Markotić.
- *Legends of Tongue* was aired on CKUA Radio, Edmonton.
- *Bestiary* was conceived as part of an art and performance exhibition entitled *Writing from Desire* held at the Winnipeg Art Gallery.
- *String Quartet* was performed at the 1995 *Loud and Queer* festival in Edmonton.
- Poems from *For Breath & Glass* were televised on The Women's Television Network, as part of the *Writing on the Wall* series.
- *Days of Water* won a silver medal in the National Magazine Awards.

My grateful thanks to the Manitoba Arts Council, the Manitoba Writers' Guild and to the Banff School of the Arts for grants that provided me with the time to write. As well my thanks to St. John's College and Library, and The Roasting House, Corydon Avenue, for high windows, coffee and light.

I would like to gratefully acknowledge my enormous debt to Don Coles and Nicole Markotić for their editorial suggestions. This catalogue would not have been complete without the following kind writers and generous readers who alternately encouraged and scolded: Dennis Cooley, Debra Dudek, Robert Gray, Susan Holloway, Cynthia Jordan, Brian Slon, Ted St. Godard, Andris Taskans, and Fred Wah.
And to my family, *con molto affetto*, with thanks.

Méira Cook was born and raised in Johannesburg, South Africa. She immigrated to Canada in 1990, and now lives in Winnipeg, where she is currently working on her doctorate in Canadian literature. Her first book, *A Fine Grammar of Bones*, was published by Turnstone Press in 1993; *the ruby garrote*, a chapbook, was published by disOrientations Press of Calgary in 1994. Her poems have appeared in such magazines and anthologies as *Border Crossings, Prairie Fire, The Fiddlehead, Vintage '93, Vintage '94, The Malahat Review* and *West Coast Line*.

TED ST. GODARD